Suffering with Christ

30 Days

Pierce Beigh

ISBN 979-8-88751-921-0 (paperback)
ISBN 979-8-88751-922-7 (digital)

Christian Faith Publishing
832 Park Avenue
Meadville, PA 16335
www.christianfaithpublishing.com

Printed in the United States of America

Preface

This book of daily devotions is dedicated to those that are suffering from chronic illness, health issues, and the overwhelming nature of life while going through trials. I wrote this to provide encouragement and hope for you while experiencing suffering. Although these devotions mainly center on chronic illness, I believe that anyone going through suffering of any type whether mental, physical, or emotional, will benefit.

You wake up today realizing that you still have the same nagging symptoms that you had three weeks ago, a month ago, and then a year ago. The same emotional distress, same mental distress, and the very same negative attitude. *What is happening to me?* You push through.

Friends begin to see you missing events and just becoming distant in general. You push harder. You make sure you're not missing out on living your life, but everything is becoming hazy. Work is not enjoyable and a challenge to get through the day. Friday seems like a miracle has arrived, only to sleep away the weekend in preparation for Monday. Your social time is spent slogging through phone calls with friends who don't really understand why you're not yourself. Eventually, you find yourself doing two things, working, and sleeping. You're unfulfilled, anxious, depressed, and in need of change. Sick and scared of the future, you ask, Where do I go? Where do I turn?

Suffering can be debilitating. Whether it's chronic illness, divorce, financial setbacks, or terminal cancer; the mind, body, and spirit are all individually yet connectively affected. It hurts to speak, think, move, and live. People wonder why you can't just be more engaging or be more positive and upbeat like you used to be! It's just not that easy.

Sometimes you give your best effort to be present and fulfilling to other people, only to find out it pushes you further down into your illness due to the fatigue and lack of energy. It takes enormous amounts of energy for a suffering person to be present in life.

Regardless of the job you have or how much money you make, if your health is suffering, nothing else seems to matter. Chronic illness makes you feel like there is nothing to live for, nothing to enjoy, and nothing to hope for. Suffering can get the best of you but only if you let it.

Suffering doesn't make sense. It isn't logical, and trying to make sense of it on your own is a losing battle. It is a vivid hourly, daily, real-life struggle. After many of your friends have stopped calling and your family seems tired of hearing about your problems, you will be left alone with a choice. You can fight this alone, desperately trying to find answers, or you can completely surrender to the Creator of the universe and team up with Him to continue and fight for answers. Neither choice guarantees good health, but one choice will mold you into the person He created you to be.

Here is my chronic illness story. I was a leader in my community and a college graduate working in the timber industry on a fast track to becoming a logging manager. I had worked as a logger for a few years before I began transitioning into management. At the age of twenty-four, I began managing logging crews for the largest timberland owner in the US and was put on a track for movement. I was making great money for my age at a fast-paced job with big machinery, wildlife, and lots of time in the woods—everything I loved.

I began to get sick. I kept pushing and pushing through my illness, hoping to get better. I was regularly skipping work to see doctors and specialists; I began to really suffer. Life was slowly winding down to a halt. After two years of suffering and slogging through my life, I decided I had to leave the job and pursue getting healthy.

As I write these devotionals, I am still sick and fighting to get a grip on this chronic illness. I know now just how dependent I am on the Lord Jesus Christ. I write these devotionals from a relationship standpoint where I am in full surrender to Jesus and His plan for my life. Jesus died for my sins on the cross, rose again, and lives on high at God's right hand. I believe that He is the author of all life, the Creator of heaven and earth, and He holds my plans, life, and future in His hands.

Although these devotions are centered toward the believer in Christ, I believe anyone searching for answers regarding suffering can benefit from reading them. If you haven't given your life over to Christ, I urge you to do so. Accept the free gift of salvation from God and begin moving in the direction He intended for you to go. Although you will not be guaranteed a perfect life, you will be given a life full of peace, joy, and hope.

Everyone suffers in one way or another. Comparing your levels of suffering to other people's is not beneficial and does not bring anything good. Your suffering is your story, my suffering is my story. I urge you to give your suffering to Christ, walk with him through your battles. He will daily take your burden and use it for your own good and His glory.

Whether you've been suffering for ten years, ten days, or ten minutes, I hope you find peace and hope in these daily assurances of Jesus Christ working in us through our sufferings.

Day 1

Christ suffered for you.

—1 Peter 2:21

Jesus Christ literally feels your pain. He feels everything you are going through. He feels your aches, your anxiety, your depressed spirit, and even your debilitating headaches. He does not just acknowledge them, He feels them with you. It hurts Him to know that you are hurting, but He knows the bigger picture, the outcome, the end of the story. His way is perfect, and this is His plan for your life.

For the believer in Christ, "all your circumstances are in the hand of God, therefore never think it strange concerning the circumstances you are in"—Oswald Chambers (*My Utmost for His Highest*, 1926).

When we are suffering at our worst, we can take heart in realizing that Christ suffered for us. Not only did He live as a man and feel our pain, but He paid the ultimate price of suffering for us. He has a plan for our suffering, and if we trust Him with the reins, He will lead us to a more glorious place than we could have ever pictured. The things you are feeling in your suffering right now were felt by the Creator of the world. You are not alone. Jesus Christ, the Author of life, feels your pain.

Carriage and rigging flying high over the unit.
Carriage: Wheeled device that rides back and forth on
the skyline and from which logs are suspended.

Day 2

There is a time for everything.

—Ecclesiastes 3:1

Solomon goes on to say there is a time to heal, a time to stay still, a time to move, and a time to be silent. In our present sufferings, it feels that life has been put on pause. We are not making any progress with our plans or moving toward our goals. Instead we seem to be treading water just to stay afloat, while everyone else seems to swim quickly by toward the future.

When playing music, counting the rests is just as important as playing the notes. Patiently counting the rests tells you when to come back in for your important part. If you lose concentration and miscount the rests, you could come back in at the wrong time and ruin the song! It is the same way with God working in this period of your life. This may be a season of "rests" for you where you take a seat and count the rests. Make sure you stay focused on the rest and not try to come back in to soon. Coming back in too soon could send you back to the beginning and cause you to lose the ground you gained. There is a reason for this suffering, and this season will eventually pass.

Remember that God is bigger than your suffering, and in His time of seasons, He will lead you if you abide in Him. Don't cheat this season and launch too soon, take the time to rest and abide. There is a time for everything.

Day 3

Apart from me you can do nothing.

—John 15:5

Imagine going through this struggle with no hope. No hope of getting better, being in love, making memories, and having joy in life. No hope of moving past this trial into a more refined and chiseled person. It is a depressing reality.

Hope keeps us moving forward, hope gets us out of bed on our worst days, and hope puts our eyes on the horizon. Without hope, there can be nothing to live for. You can't do anything without hope.

Thank God for His son Jesus. Jesus is our hope! Putting our hope in Jesus is trusting the creator of the world to hold your future, your breath, and your life in his hand. There is no hope without Jesus, but with Jesus our hope is renewed daily. He is the reason we keep on pushing, grinding, and moving forward. This world places hope in people and possessions, things that won't last or fulfill our deepest desires. Jesus will fulfill those desires and overflow you with hope during this season of suffering. Even during the most painful moments, we can have peace through our hope in Jesus.

Sometimes it feels your trial has not improved even though you are doing everything right with regards to your relationship with Christ. Keep pressing on, keep grinding, have hope. Is there a better alternative? Is there a better place to put your hope? There isn't. Remember that God is bigger than your trial; He will pull you through in His timing.

In the words of Desmond Doss, a World War II (WWII) hero who rescued wounded soldiers from the battlefield in the Pacific Islands, "One more, Lord, give me one more." As the days get long and your hope diminishes, ask Christ to give you the strength to get one more.

One more hour, Lord—one more day, one more week, and sometimes just one more minute—let me put all the hope I have into You and Your plan for my life.

Day 4

*My present sufferings are not worth comparing
with the glory that will be revealed in us.*

—Romans 8:18

This too shall pass. It might pass like a golf ball-sized kidney stone, but it will pass. When it does, how amazing will that be! You will have a closer relationship with Jesus and a new appreciation for life and good health.

Isn't it wild to think that even though we are in all this pain at the moment, the glory revealed later will be better? In fact, it will be so much better it won't even be worth comparing to our sufferings. Now we might not see this glory till we are in heaven; it might not happen in our lifetime. It is hard to grasp that we could suffer greatly for a long time during our time on this earth, but if we have Jesus on our side, He guarantees that our suffering will not be worth comparing to the glory.

I believe this glory revealed in us can be for other people to enjoy also. Perhaps you're struggling so hard right now but have pushed through the pain each day and tried to live out your faith in spite of your circumstances. Well, I guarantee someone is watching you. Someone is taking notes, someone is learning from you, and perhaps even growing closer to Christ through your struggles. So these seasons of suffering and pain might not always be for the sufferer but for the onlooker and friends as well. Perhaps your suffering is not only for you but for someone else close to you. Remember that God is always bigger.

Log truck getting loaded before first light.

Day 5

I have learned to be content whatever the circumstances…I can do everything through Christ who gives me strength.

—Philippians 4:11 and 13

It is pretty hard to be content during this period of life. Everyone else is smiling, laughing, and carrying on with life; I'm here just trying to get through the day without collapsing. The last thing I am is content!

We must remember that God is bigger and this is His plan, this is your story. In a bad storm, you have to go with what you know and not what you feel. We may feel that God is far from us, but we know that is not true.

There is a balance between accepting where God has you at the moment and fighting to move forward to where God wants you to be. We cannot sit entirely idle and wait for God to make a move, but we must be content with our circumstances while actively pursuing a solution with God. Take action but also be content. It seems like a double standard.

Being content is not the same as being lazy and giving up. "Godliness with contentment is great gain (1 Timothy 6:6)." If we begin to be content with our circumstances and appreciate the opportunity to suffer with Christ, then we will begin to see that all things are possible through Christ Jesus, who gives us strength. This will allow us to move forward.

Day 6

Forgetting what is behind and straining toward what is ahead, I press on toward the prize for which God has called me in Christ Jesus.

—Philippians 3:13–14

Maybe you left a job over this suffering. Perhaps you lost friendships, relationships, and community due to your trials. It's easy for us to look back and see all that has gone wrong—all that we have lost or missed out on. But when we do, we lose focus on the goal and purpose. The past will take our attention away from the present and the future, hurting us more than we realize. It's important to look at the past to help us with the future, but getting stuck in what-if scenarios, and wishing things would have been different, does not help you to move forward in any way.

Paul says that in order to press on toward what God has called us to do, we must leave the past and only look ahead. In chronic illness or suffering, it is hard not to let the previous days, months, or even years drag you down in the present moment. Suffering tends to compound itself over time, making it even more difficult to move forward. At some point, maybe even believing that the pain is too much to remove and moving forward isn't an option.

But we must move forward, each day is a fresh slate. In the words of John Wayne:

> Tomorrow is the most important thing in life.
> Comes into us at midnight very clean. It's perfect
> when it arrives, and it puts itself in our hands.
> It hopes we've learned something from yesterday.

We need to remind ourselves each morning that the past is history; pressing on toward what God has called you is what is important right now. No matter your level of suffering, remember to press on toward the prize each day. It will be worth it, God promises.

Day 7

His mercies are new every morning.

—Lamentations 3:23

What an awesome thing to comprehend. Every day is a new year, a clean slate, a fresh start. We don't get new mercies each Monday and have to use them wisely throughout the week, we get them new daily. In fact, Christ's mercies are new at each moment throughout the day, but to us, the morning signifies a complete fresh start. Remember this after you've had a terrible day of pain or suffering. Tomorrow is a new day full of his mercies all over again; nothing you can do will change that. Suffering has a way of dragging us down and down and down, until we don't think we can climb out of the hole. Sometimes the best thing we can do at the end of a long day of suffering is to just go to bed and wake up with new mercies.

It is important to remember that we must confess our sins in order to receive new mercies at any moment. No matter how bad your suffering has been, restoring your relationship with Jesus is vital. Throw your sins and burdens on the cross and let them be replaced with fresh joy, love, and mercies. Every morning is a new batch of grace and mercy.

Getting to the tower at sunrise ready to work. Summertime.

Day 8

Be still and know that I am God.

—Psalm 46:10

"Be still" does not mean be inactive, or slow, or lazy. It means to keep your heart still. We can still be active throughout each day, yet at the same time, remain "still." It is a matter of heart, not of movement. Throughout our trial we can take heart knowing that God is the beginning and the end, the creator, the king, the master, and the author of life. This should cause us to stop and just be still, realizing that He is Lord over all things. How can we not trust Him with this season of suffering?

The world says to fight it on your own, search for the answers, see multiple doctors, find what makes you happy, and go after that, etc. Not that those are bad things, but they can take our focus off God. What we really need to do is to be still, and recognize that God is God of all and He is in control. Then these things will come into focus as to which doctor to see and how to move forward.

The context of this verse was rooted in the unknown of what might happen. The writer was in place where everything was shaking around him, and the only thing solid was God's consistency. The one thing that kept the unknown future tolerable was knowing God was his refuge and strength.

It is so easy to work ourselves up and get moving so fast that we don't see the overall picture and plan. Slowing down to speed up is the key, and being still is the way to get there. In the most painful days, we can remember and apply to our lives what this psalm says, "Be still and know that I am God."

Heading over the hill to set chokers at sunrise. Wintertime.

*Consider it pure joy whenever you face trials of many kinds,
because you know that the testing of your faith develops
perseverance. Perseverance must finish its work so that you
may be mature and complete, not lacking anything.*

—James 1:2–3

It can seem impossible to look suffering in the eye and squeeze pure joy from it. That can be the last thing you think of when going through trials. Think of it this way: you are an ordinary piece of iron that God saw worthy to mold into something he deemed beautiful. In order to mold iron, you must place it in the furnace until it's so hot, it can bend easily and form to what the maker wants. Once the iron is smoldering hot, it is taken out and beaten profusely to bend and twist to the maker's specifications. Once the piece is molded, it is then cooled and the outcome is a beautiful masterpiece.

If we trust God through our suffering, we are just like the piece of iron in the fire. If we persevere through the trial and continue to look up the other side will be amazing—a molded masterpiece. God says so Himself!

The longer you are in this fire, the more molding there is to be done. In other words, the longer the Lord's hand lingers over you, the more beautiful the outcome will be. If we daily trust in God's plan through this trial, He will see us to a more purposeful future beyond our own plans.

Break time. Putting my feet up on the D8 CAT during a unit change.

Day 10

He must become greater; I must become less.

—John 3:30

Throughout this suffering in your life, it's obvious that you have become less. But have you made God bigger?

I get on a one-track mind sometimes and think about me, me, me. How *my* suffering is painful and how *my* life is rough. Sometimes you absolutely must put yourself first in order to heal and eventually be better for others, but in no circumstances should you put yourself first before God.

Even while we are going through this excruciating trial, we can still give glory to God and put Him first through our pain. You're probably wondering how since most days you barely have enough energy to do the tasks at hand. Well, it's the little things. For starters, deeply accept that this is a trial allowed directly from God himself and that your situation and future are completely held in his hand. Knowing and firmly believing this will allow you to stand on solid ground throughout the earthquake. It will also change your heart and attitude toward the circumstances. Slowly, you will see how you react differently to people when talking about your ailments. Talking about yourself will not seem so fulfilling anymore.

Suffering can develop great empathy and compassion in us. Seeing the world, our circumstances, and other people through the eyes of Christ and not through our own eyes, will make us want to make God bigger and ourselves smaller.

He is there with us going through our trials, giving us the strength to continue if we look to Him. Acknowledge God's greatness, that He is always bigger, through any suffering or trial.

Nice tower setting. If you look closely, you can see 3 towers in the picture.

Day 11

My grace is sufficient for you, for my power is made perfect in weakness.

—2 Corinthians 12:9

I need the right doctor! I need the right medication to feel better. I need a counselor and the right friends to help me through this. I need to get my life back. Yes, all those things are needed, and in due time, will come along. But if all those things never came, how would we respond?

His grace is sufficient; we need not ask for anything more. This does not mean that we should sit back and not take action to improve our situation, but we should reflect daily with the realization that His grace is enough.

What does it mean that His grace is enough? It's probably a little different for every person going through a trial, but to me, it means that no matter what this world does to us, it cannot take away Christ from my heart. The world cannot take away the place we have in heaven because of God's Grace. His grace is all we need.

Chokers dangling from the carriage above rainier.
Chokers: Long heavy cables that are attached around logs via choker setters down in the brush, then pulled up by the carriage to the landing.

Day 12

—Isaiah 40:31

We all know this verse. We've either seen it written somewhere or spoken at the closing words in a sermon to really send the message home. But what does it mean to wait upon the Lord? What does it mean to wait upon the Lord when you are laid low and going through seemingly unending trials? I believe it means something a little different for everyone going through trials. For me, it means to literally wait, to trust God and His plan while I stand idle, unable to move forward. When the Lord allows you to be laid low, however it may be, it's for a reason. A reason we don't know now and perhaps will not ever know. But we cannot forget that there is a purpose to our sufferings, and we must stay obedient to God during the storm in order to see our own purpose fulfilled through Him.

Maybe you've lost your marriage, your job, someone close passed away, depressed with life, or just lost hope recently and not sure why; for me it's been a chronic health crisis. My job, health, social life, and independence were taken away from me. It seemed like I was justified to have every reason to be mad at God and frustrated with His plan! I was much like Joseph in the Old Testament, who had all the reason to be angry. But there is a purpose, and if I stay committed to the path, I will see it too fruition.

So what does waiting on the Lord look like? Pastor Paul Sheppard said it best with these three things. When you are laid LOW, you must use your time to

> *L—Learn.* God put you in this position for a reason. Learn what that is. Dig deep, expand. Read, pray, and pursue like you've never done before.

> *O—Obey.* Be obedient to God even though you want to throw it all away. Obedience is key to keeping yourself unpolluted and able to live the future God has planned for you.

> *W—Worship.* Worship God during this period. He is the God of the hills and of the valleys. Worship Him during your deepest valleys.

When you come out of this trial, which you will, you will be better equipped spiritually, emotionally, and mentally to serve God and spread His word. Wait upon the Lord.

Timber is all cut and ready to be brought to the landing. Tough
logging on a long layout. Tower in top right is 110 ft tall for scale.

Day 13

All things work together for good for those who love him.

—Romans 8:28

Wow, it sure doesn't seem that way does it. When will it end? When will my suffering, physical and emotional pain, and situational depression end? Will I ever see the life I once lived, or get to fulfill the future I had pictured in my mind? It is hard to believe that what I am going through is a good thing. It doesn't feel good to me. I cannot believe that this is supposed to be good. Sometimes, reading Bible verses like this one do not really seem to solve or help anything. I still am suffering greatly and cannot see or feel anything good coming from it.

This verse is the words of the Creator of the universe, and if He says "What you're going through is a good thing," well then, I better believe it. This verse takes faith! I don't want to be in this place. I would give anything, absolutely anything, to get my health back and be on my way. God has other plans; He has something better, something bigger, something more good than what I can comprehend with my small brain.

The reality of the situation is, if you believe in Jesus and have put your faith in Him, whatever you go through is for your personal benefit and the benefit of others. So keep slogging through the mud. Keep waking up each day and pushing, pushing forward. Even when you are so irritable and angry with your situation that you can't be around anyone else, keep pushing. Because remember, all things work together for good in Jesus.

Day 14

I press on toward the goal to win the prize for which
God has called me heavenward in Christ Jesus.

—Philippians 3:14

Keep your eye on the prize. I just got off the phone with my diesel automotive technician telling me I need a new motor. I took my truck in about a week ago to get a small complaint of a rough idle looked at. I thought it might be a bad injector or a faulty sensor creating the smoke and rough idle, nothing huge really. After spending $3,500 on what was supposed to fix the problem, nothing was different. Turns out I need a new motor, and the bill would be $10k. It felt like the punches just didn't stop.

This is just an example of a truck. My health journey has been tenfold the importance of a truck, but events like this can easily take our eyes off the prize and lead us into bitterness and resentment.

We must walk through life realizing and understanding that circumstances do not determine our joy and salvation. They can definitely add or subtract to our happiness, there is no doubt about that, but we should continually be looking forward to Jesus, to his calling and purpose. The enemy's goal is for us to take our eyes off Jesus. He will go to any lengths to make that happen. No matter the obstacles or situation that we find ourselves in, we must press on toward the goal in Christ Jesus.

Timber cutters bore into an old dangerous snag
that had to be fell before logging occurred.

Day 15

*When pride comes, then comes disgrace, but
with humility comes wisdom.*

—Proverbs 11:2

Life changes, that's a fact. In order to be present, you must learn to adapt to those changes and overcome them as the new normal. But what happens when the change is one you just can't swallow? For instance, you lose your job as an important executive and are now drawing unemployment. People who once respected you and looked up to you and your position are now giving their glances to someone else. Your pride is shattered. You feel that your self-worth is low. From a worldly aspect, you have really taken a backseat. You need to get back in the grind and work your way back up so people will notice you. But from a godly perspective, maybe this is the correct order of events. Not maybe, it is!

I am currently unemployed because of my health issues, and as a man with strong abilities and ambitions, it is incredibly demoralizing. It is especially sad when friends are doing amazing things, working multiple jobs, and call you in the middle day to see how you are doing only to find you don't have anything to tell because you're not able to be active in this stage of life. It hurts, hurts your pride.

This verse tells us that with humility comes wisdom. I trust God for my current situation, and I will push aside my pride to deal with my situation in a biblical way. As tough as it might be, when you are laid low, you must focus on Christ and His plan and not returning to yourself to regain your status and worldly pride. His plan is better.

Day 16

In this world you will find trouble, but take heart! I have overcome the world.

—John 16:33

Life is hard at best, am I right? Finding trouble is a guarantee in this world. It can come in many different forms from health and sickness to just plain bad circumstances that happened regardless of anything you did. Sometimes it can seem like no matter what you do, you just can't win at life. We all know the saying "When life gives you lemons, make lemonade." Well sometimes life gives you lemons then life continues to throw lemons at you while you're down and makes you choke on the lemon juice until you can't breathe. Then life just laughs and continues throwing lemons at you while you're choking on your knees. Wouldn't it have been better to just make lemonade?

I believe it's how you react to the beatdown that God is really interested in. This is boot camp. You want to build some character and become a better-equipped Christian, father, mother, brother or sister, or spouse? Well then you better be ready for life to throw you some beanballs, and you better be ready to get up and glorify God regardless of your pain and situation.

No matter the situation, we can still take heart in knowing that Jesus Christ has overcome any worldly situation that we find ourselves in. If we turn to Him and cast our situations and emotions toward Him and His plan, we will come out better and more like him on the other side. Take heart; He has overcome the world.

Day 17

If God is for us, who can be against us.

—Romans 8:31

In our current state of anguish (whether chronic illness, personal issues, or just plain life issues) we can sometimes lose track of God. Perhaps for one week you didn't pick up your Bible because you were feeling too crummy to read, and soon that week turns into two weeks. You soon find yourself becoming more upset and angrier at people around you and the world in general. You're thinking, *What on earth, is this a new symptom?* Yes, it is! It is a symptom of a lessened relationship with your Creator, which is a big deal.

I do not want to undermine your physical condition though, as anger or irritability can most definitely be new symptoms that develop over time, as I have personally experienced. But my point is that even just a little Bible reading or talking with God daily can do wonders for our spirit, mind, and body. It will help with our illnesses and problems in every way. God will work through our minds and hearts to heal us mentally, spiritually, and physically.

Talking to God each day also gives us a glimmer of hope. We may not begin to feel better physically after we spend time with him, but we will have hope and peace regarding our situation. Remember to talk to God, and give Him you're suffering and problems today. He will make sense of them.

Day 18

In your anger do not sin.

—Ephesians 4:26

When we are angry and emotionally down, what do we do? Well, we usually say things we don't mean, act in ways we don't normally act, and we do things we don't normally do. When we are angry and upset, we usually resort to sin and we justify it due to our circumstance. We look for a way out, an answer to the problem, an instant gratification perhaps, all while not realizing the detrimental effects it has on ourselves as well as others.

Why not though, right? We are down and out, nothing's going our way, and we're already down in the pit; why not just stay here? Wrong. In your anger, do not sin! It will make you angrier and farther from the exit of the pit.

The devil has a great way of enticing us with sinful things when we are already in a vulnerable state. He wants you to take the bait with hopes it will make you feel better, and sometimes it will, but only for a fleeting moment and the consequences will outweigh the benefits.

Whatever you do, do not sin in this state of your life. Remember that this is not your destination; keep the faith and keep moving onward and upward. Do this so that God's plan with your life can be fulfilled to the max and not derailed by a sinful fork in the road.

Day 19

When Job's three friends heard about all the troubles that had come upon him, they set out from their homes and met together by agreement to go and sympathize with him and comfort him.

—Job 2:11

Job had some friends. His friends showed up, saw just how much pain Job was in, and sat there for seven days and nights with him without saying a word. *Wow.* Don't we all know how sweet it is for a friend to care? They don't have to have the solution, or even attempt to have one, but just to show they care.

In your current state of illness or suffering, it is important to remember to call on friends to share your burden. Of course we can throw everything suffering-related at the feet of Jesus and He will take care of it, but Jesus also gave us friends in this world to help us through life. Do not be afraid to be truthful with your friends about your suffering and current problems. True friends will walk with you through your mud, they won't use it against you, and they sure won't spread rumors about you. They will be there with you through the mud and into the sun.

Chronic illness and suffering in general can make you feel isolated in many aspects both mentally and socially. Friendship breaks that isolation and brings hope back into our hearts. Reach out today to a close friend and ask for care. If they do not know about your exact level of suffering, they will have no way to accurately pray and care for you. Friends are the best.

A turn of logs goes to the landing as the rigging crew watches. The rigging crew in this picture consists of two choker setters and a rigging slinger. The rigging slinger is the boss of the choker setters and tells them with logs to choke. It can be quite tricky as logs can be on top of each other all which ways. As well as picking out turns he is responsible for the safety of the crew in the brush. A machine on the landing is ready for the logs.

Day 20

Blessed is the man you discipline, O Lord.

—Psalm 94:12

The Lord disciplines the one He loves. Endure hardship
as discipline; God is treating you as his children.

—Hebrews 12:6–7

It seems to me that there are two types of discipline: correction and preparation. No one really likes either type of discipline, because they are uncomfortable and require growing pains. *Correction* is when your current situation is directly related to your past actions or behaviors. The Lord does not necessarily "punish" us for our past sins, but He will allow things in our life that reflect our past actions—cause and effect. Mainly, you may not see the blessings you were hoping for. But as the verse says, "Blessed is the man you discipline," so consider it a blessing if you are uncomfortable in your walk. It means the Lord is calling you to a closer relationship and has extraordinary things for you to do in your future. It is crucial to throw your past at the cross and begin moving onwards and upwards.

The other type of discipline is *preparation*. This is when suffering and illness come unexpectedly. Nothing you do could prevent it and there is nothing you can immediately do to change it. The Lord is preparing you; you are in boot camp. He is using this suffering season to mold you and build your character into the person He created you to be. So in the middle of your current suffering, take time to say, "Thank you, Lord, thank you for choosing me for this suffering." Just as the Lord saw Job fit for the suffering he endured because of his faithfulness, so it is the same with suffering for the believer. The Bible shows us that the more suffering we endure the greater use the Lord has for us.

Day 21

We rejoice in our sufferings because we know that suffering produces perseverance, perseverance character, and character hope.

—Romans 5:3

We have all heard someone say "That builds character," when a kid falls and scrapes his knee, but what about building character through suffering as an adult? Perhaps you have a problem with substance abuse or a loved one has an addiction that you cannot seem to help. Maybe you are struggling through a chronic illness or proceeding through a divorce as a single parent now. If we are dependent on the Lord through our suffering, we wholeheartedly know that our suffering is not in vain; it is for our gain and God's glory!

Our present suffering will produce perseverance, determination, and momentum to keep going and move forward. Our perseverance will build character, and our character will give us hope to tackle another day. Our hope will strengthen our lives for future trials, and it will spread to other people's lives and affect them in positive ways. So as painful as it can be, take your suffering and rejoice in it. The character you will build through these trials will be far greater than anything you would have built without them.

However, this will only produce lasting character if we give our suffering to God and let him take control. If we try to do things on our own, suffering will in fact produce more suffering, and we may become bitter and hopeless, which is exactly the opposite of what God wants for your life. In order to live the full life God has planned for you, keep looking up at Him during this period of your life. He will develop your character into the godly person He made you to be.

A choker setter looks over the timber as logs go to the landing.

Day 22

We do not lose heart.

—2 Corinthians 4:1

Take heart. If you lose your heart, you lose the battle. So what does it mean to take heart? It means to believe that your full situation is in the hands of Jesus Christ. I also believe it means to saddle up and prepare for the road ahead. It's time to dig deep. Johnny Cash says it best:

> You're gonna have to get some gravel in ya guts,
> and spit in yer eye.

It's time to tackle the suffering like a rigging man tackles the tangled chokers on a rainy day in the woods; with strength, a good attitude, and pure determination.

The world will throw obstacle after obstacle at you, forcing you to get some grit in your heart and perseverance in your step. As Jesus said, "In this world you will find trouble, but take heart, I have overcome the world" (John 16:33). We must build mental muscle memory throughout our trials and suffering. Digging into the deepest parts of our spirit and believing that we can do this, we will get through this, and we will overcome this.

Amid your present suffering, dig deep into your spirit and give it a pep rally. Take heart knowing that you can overcome this! It's going to take tears, sweat, and the blood of Jesus, but you will come out of this. If we take heart in the Lord, there is nothing that we cannot face.

Day 23

*Get rid of all bitterness, rage and anger, brawling
and slander, along with every form of malice.*

—Ephesians 4:31

Bitterness can creep up over time without us knowing. Our long-term suffering can create resentment toward people who don't understand. It can create bitterness toward past employers or even bitterness toward doctors who could not help or, perhaps, misdiagnosed our condition. We may not be an outwardly bitter person, and think we are not inwardly as well, but bitterness can ooze out through a crack and become present to others without us realizing.

Granted there are symptoms of various illnesses that cause anger, hostility, irritability, and bitterness for the time being. So I do not want to undermine the physiological symptoms one might be feeling, but we must be able to separate symptoms from actual feelings which can be extremely hard to do.

It's hard to just "get rid" of all bitterness after what you have gone through but it must be done. We must acknowledge that this was God's plan for our life all along, every step of the journey. If we commit to his plan and follow His word, we will soon see all bitterness in our hearts fade away. God is always bigger than our situation and bitterness.

Day 24

How many are your works, O Lord! In wisdom you made them all.

—Psalm 104:24

I can get tunnel vision especially when going through dark trials. We focus on our situation, our suffering, and our problems. We forget to look around, look at others, and sometimes even forget to step outside and enjoy the sunny day. Of course, in order to get well and to be there for others there has to be some serious focus on ourselves. But we cannot forget how important it is to stop and look around at all the wonders God has made. Creation itself is healing. Being barefoot outside on a crisp fall day will help with your headaches. Walking down by the calm creek will help with your anxiety. Watching a herd of elk feed through the clear-cut, as the sun goes down, will give you hope for the hunting years ahead. God's creations are there for us to enjoy in so many ways. They occupy our minds with the present wonder yet allow us peace and tranquility to think logically and move forward.

Becoming healthy and ending your current trials is not as simple as just "getting outside." But looking at the bigger picture, with God's works in the center, will allow you to understand your situation better and move forward to where He wants you to be. Praise God for His amazing works! During our darkest suffering, we can always praise God for His awesome power and wisdom in creation.

Log loader waiting for the next truck to arrive. Summertime sunrise; above the fog looking out towards the ocean.

Day 25

The Father of compassion and the God of comfort, who comforts us in all our troubles, so that we can comfort those in any trouble with the comfort we ourselves received from God.

—2 Corinthians 1:4

How often do we find that someone else is going through something just as debilitating as us? All the time. It may not be as serious to you but it is to them. Although during this season of our own suffering, there may not be much we can give in regard to emotional help but just acknowledging their trial and showing them you care can be everything needed. Isn't that all that we need during our own suffering? We can surely show we care by pointing them to the God of comfort, the Father of compassion. How incredible!

Perhaps this season of suffering in your life is preparing you to help other people in a similar state of suffering. You will have been through the fire and know what it takes to get through. You will know just how emotionally wrecking suffering can be. Only then will you be able to be the comfort to someone greatly suffering, pointing to the ultimate comforter, Jesus Christ. You have already seen the incredible compassion of the Father during your suffering and soon you will be able to show it to someone else. Show them comfort just like the comfort you received from God and you will impact lives for eternity.

In your season of suffering, do not find comfort in things that will let you down; continue to look up to the great healer for comfort and compassion.

Day 26

—Psalm 95:1

Music has a way of uplifting our spirit like nothing else can. Whether it's listening to worship music in the morning to start the day or pretending you have a great voice while singing along loudly in the car, music will give you the extra boost to get through the day. Music has been a large part of my life and an even bigger part of my illness recovery. Sometimes there is nothing else that can give you that edge feeling besides music.

God created music for our enjoyment. He also created it as a means for us to praise Him. Use music to both praise God and to heal. Memorize praise tunes in your head and replay them over and over, it will change your attitude. When you find yourself listening to music and praising God, you will see your outlook on your trials slowly change. The music will uplift your spirit and the praise will strengthen your faith in God and his plan for your life. So crank some tunes!

Day 27

The prayer of a righteous man is powerful and effective.

—James 5:16

We don't always get the answer we want when we pray, but we know it is the right answer. God is never wrong!

Sometimes we feel there is nowhere else to go. We have checked all the boxes, talked to all the right people, seen all the best doctors, and still, we are in the midst of our suffering. From a worldly standpoint, there *is* nowhere else to go. But from a heavenly standpoint, the only place we can go is to our knees in prayer. When all seems lost, fall on your knees and pour your heart out to the God who loves you and deeply feels what you are going through. Abraham Lincoln said it best.

> I have been driven many times upon my knees by
> the overwhelming conviction that I had nowhere
> else to go.

He said this amid the heat of the Civil War. When there is nothing else to do and nothing seems to help, keep praying.

Many times it will seem like your prayers are not answered or they are not heard. We know this not to be true. We must keep opening the gates of heaven with our prayers. They are heard and God is working. Pour them on each day; give Him your thoughts and needs daily. With a close relationship with Christ, your prayer is powerful and effective and answers will come in God's timing.

Day 28

"Be strong and work, for I am with you," declared the Lord.

—Haggai 2:4

There's no free ride. No one said it'd be easy. Suck
it up, tough it out, and be the best you can.

—John Cougar Mellencamp

We all want an answer now. We want the Lord to come down and just solve our problems Himself. We want to be healed right this second. Don't get me wrong, He is absolutely capable of that. And if that is His will, it'll happen that way. Other times, while the Lord is with you through it, you are going to have to get active and pursue a solution. It's not going to be easy and it's going to require a lot of work, hard work. This type of work comes from the heart; it uses your mind, body, and spirit. It will take mental toughness to keep going, physical strength to not give up, and a grounded spirit in Christ to continue to have hope. Although the Lord is with us every step, we must personally buckle the seat belt and get moving. Sometimes you must put your head down and work, all while knowing that the Lord is with you and guiding your steps.

Be strong and work. He is with us the whole way.

Day 29

But as for you, be strong and do not give up,
for your work will be rewarded.

—2 Chronicles 15:7

Don't give up! It's going to take everything you've got, but it will be worth it. Anything that's worth something takes time and effort.

Isn't that just the best thing to hear from someone, "Don't give up"? When someone tells you that, it gives you a little morsel of hope, drive, and push. It gives your heart the extra effort to dig just a little more. In logging, on the hottest of days with little water, all that's on your mind is quittin' time. When your hook tender says, "Almost quittin' time, fellas. Don't give up, let's get a few more loads out," that lights a fire under you. Just those little words of encouragement can change everything.

We get those words, "Don't give up," directly from the word of God. How much more do they mean there than from fellow man? He tells us that it's worth it; it will not be in vain. There is a plan for our suffering, one we cannot see. It is so important that we do not give up. Our lives depend on it, and think about how many other lives and futures depend on you not giving up. Other people's futures are directly tied to you not giving up. Think about that one.

If we continue to look to God for strength and not give up, He will bless us on the other side of this trial.

Day 30

A good name is more desirable than great riches;
to be esteemed is better than silver or gold.

—Proverbs 22:1

Suffering is hard. This part of your life will soon be over and you can move toward a better future filled with happiness, more joy, less suffering, and many of the things that you couldn't enjoy before! Once we are on the other side, looking back, what will we see? Personally, I will remember how much the suffering took from me, how terrible it was, and how I wouldn't want anyone I know or love to experience it. I will look back and see all the days of toil and sleepless nights wishing my suffering would end. I will see how my anxious and depressed spirit, over the last years, has molded me into the man I am becoming today. I will see how the daily pain of living with a disease allowed my character to become expanded and solidified into a godly man. Looking back will allow me to see God's hand through it all, how He led me into the fire, and how He miraculously led me out.

But while looking back, what will I be able to say about how I acted? What will others say? Although during our trials of suffering it's important to not dwell on what other people say about you, it's just as important to strive to still live in a godly way for others to see. This means to take your trial from the Lord and to lean on him to get you through.

Imagine what a testimony you will be if you lived according to God's Word during your trial. You will be blessed with a good name by many and will have inspired other people going through similar trials. You just may have brought someone to Christ through the way you handled your trials. It is good to remember that someone else is always watching and learning from your season of suffering.

Make sure to remember His name while going through this trial. Remembering His name will allow you to move through this trial with purpose and come out on the other side with your name unblemished.

Me driving the skidder for a few months.

Logging unit we did on the Southwest side of Mt. Rainier.

Conclusion

God ruthlessly perfects who He royally elects.

—Skip Heitzig

I am still in my health fight as this disease has taken many things from me. As a man with ambitions and dreams to fulfill, this obstacle has shaken me to my core. If it wasn't for the Lord and His power and strength, I am sure it would have swallowed me up by now. Remember, God is always bigger than your suffering.

Pierce Beigh

About the Author

I am a born-again Christian and an avid outdoorsman who believes that all things work together for good for those who love God. This includes deep trials and suffering in life as well as a missed opportunity on that nice rainbow trout in a mountain stream. Both are experiences that, if given to God, will mold our character and produce fruit for our own lives, others' lives, and ultimately give glory to God!

I had to experience the dark valley of suffering firsthand to truly understand that God is faithful and will never leave my side. During my battle with Lyme disease, I came to a point where complete surrender to Christ was my only option. Only then did I realize that giving your life and trials fully to Christ is the only way to experience abundant life.

I now use my deep understanding of suffering to help people of all ages and backgrounds. I currently work as a fireman in the greater Seattle area.